It's Over

It's Over

Finding Freedom By Breaking Negative Strongholds

9-Week Devotional

BY

Melanie Joyce Johnson & Shanita R. Jones

www.bookstandpublishing.com

Published by
Bookstand Publishing
Morgan Hill, CA 95037
3621_8

Scriptures are KJV unless otherwise noted

ISBN 978-1-61863-263-0

Printed in the United States of America

from Melanie Joyce Johnson:

To my Heavenly Father, Creator, Provider, my Savior, who formed me in love to seek peace in this volatile world. Without your direction, this book would be non-existent. Thank you for using me to write. I love you. I owe you everything.

To my family, even through our ups and downs we're still together! To my beautiful Mom, Phyllis, thank you for teaching me that sometimes you got to laugh to keep from crying; that has really come in handy in this life. To my brothers, Jason and Lee (Jr.), I love you two like crazy. Thank you for supporting and loving me too. To my brother Chris, may you rest in peace. I miss you. To my wonderful Grandma, Martha, I thank God for you. Thank you for teaching me the gospel in your kitchen on Phillips Street and for always praying for me. You're the one lady that I know personally that still gets down on her knees and prays every morning. My, to be like you one day would be an honor.

To Shanita, my BEST friend, co-author, and sister that I never had (but can now thank God for), I love you. We've been called twins, sisters, sidekicks, road dogs, and troublemakers; yet I wouldn't want to be called any of those things if you weren't that other person. Thank you for making me laugh, from sun-up to sundown! I thank you for never giving up on me, for loving me when I was SO unlovable, for challenging me to come out of myself, and for teaching me what a strong Christian woman of God looks like. When I met you January 2, 2005, who knew that we would become friends and be writing our first book together! I thank God for you everyday.

To my spiritual family in the church of Christ, thank you for keeping me laughing and prayed up. Thank you for your support and for being there at just the right time. I thank God for the sound biblical truths and strong foundation that I've learned from many of you. I am grateful to call you brothers and sisters.

Lastly, in memory of Alphonso Gilliam Sr., thank you for teaching me what a spiritual father really looks like. I never knew what that was until I met you in Fayetteville over 6 years ago. Thank you for the looks during worship that made me laugh but also kept me in line. Thank you for your honesty, for going with me to get the Buick (smile), and for placing in me the spirit of evangelism. I miss you so very much and hope that I'm making you proud.

from Shanita R. Jones:

To my Faithful Father, my Protector, my Strength, thank you for creating me and showing me the meaning of true love. Thank you God for giving me the words to write and speak; this book is evidence of your leading in my life. Thank you for calling me to fulfill Your Purpose; without you I'm nothing.

To my family, thank you so much for your encouragement and support over the years. Thank you for the lessons learned both spoken and unspoken. To Juanita, my beautiful Mom, thanks for teaching me how to endure in this life and to never give up, I love you. To my wonderful sister Shanté, my role model, my example, my heart, I love you! I could never live without you. I thank you for showing me the true meaning of sacrifice. You mean the world to me, and I owe you my life. Happy Thanksgiving (inside joke)!

To Melanie, my best friend, and co-author, my life changed for the better when I met you. Thanks for showing me that the biblical example of friendship found in Jonathan and David is possible today. Thanks for sharing in my life; you truly are my "soul sister." Thanks for listening even when you felt like falling asleep at night, or when you had no clue what I was talking about. Thanks for being true to God and to yourself. I'm proud of you!

To my church of Christ family over the years, thanks for the strong biblical foundation that daily allows me to stay firmly planted on God's Word. Thanks for pushing me to think outside of the box; in more ways than you know. To all of my friends that have prayed for, encouraged, laughed with, and cried with me over the years, thank you. I could name you all but I'm sure I'd miss someone. If you're wondering if this is for you, yes it is!

In memory of Daddy Gilliam (Alphonso Sr.), thank you for being my spiritual father. You and Mama Gilliam took me in as one of your own. I miss you and I love you. Thanks for having an evangelistic mind that is now carried out in my life.

And last but not least, in memory of my Great Grandmother, Gertrude Howlett, thanks for introducing me to Christ. Thanks for pinching me when I acted out in church; I'm a better person today, even if I didn't understand it way back then. Thanks for teaching me how to become the hands and feet of Christ. Your legacy lives through me. Mom gave me your bible, that's the best gift I've ever received. I love you and I hope you are proud!

To our "sneak peek" reviewers, thank you for your honest feedback and critique. Thank you for investing your free time, energy, and love into this book and making suggestions on what needed to be re-written and re-worded for clarity. We appreciate you.

And to those of you who are in search of freedom this book is for you. We have made ourselves transparent and moved ourselves out of the way so that God can be clearly seen. We are praying for your release, your healing, and your renewed love for God and yourself.

x

TABLE OF CONTENTS

<u>**PURPOSE:**</u>

Sin separates us from God (Isaiah 59:2). The purpose of this 9-week devotional book is to help you be free from the chains of sin and to assist you in reconciling your relationship with God. To do this, you must be willing to take an introspective, self-examination. This requires you to become completely transparent in order to produce the spiritual freedom the Lord created you to experience. God has left His word with great examples of His love for you.

This book will be used as an avenue of encouragement. You will notice that each chapter is written with terms that reference jail or prison; this is done to show you that a relationship with satan is like being in bondage. We have given the enemy too much control over our lives and it is time to end this relationship. Satan has been angry with God ever since he was banished from heaven (Isaiah 14:12, Revelation 12:9) and it has been his sole mission ever since to keep Christians from having a wholesome relationship with God. Tell satan, "It's Over." Break up with him and be reunited with your first love, Christ.

It is our prayer that God's word, along with this devotional will help you rekindle your love relationship with the Lord! It is time to release negative strongholds! God is on your side. Do not be afraid to Trust Him; we did, and now we are on a better path to spiritual freedom!!

The Authors,
Melanie Joyce Johnson & Shanita R. Jones

<u>HOW TO USE THIS DEVOTIONAL BOOK:</u>

We are excited that you have decided to take this freedom-experiencing journey with us! This book will bring awareness to any negative strongholds you may have in your life. This 9-week, Monday through Friday, devotional is set up to give you the tools you need to fight off the enemy. There will be one lesson per week beginning on Monday that will include a weekly topic, scripture, lesson, prayer, quote, and one question per day. Each lesson is designed to help you:

1) identify and confront any negative strongholds that you may be dealing with,
2) cultivate specific prayers related to your stronghold,
3) ponder on a quote to inspire you throughout this transformation,
4) take a deep look within and reflect on the daily question provided, and
5) meditate on scriptures to help you apply the question and keep you focused throughout the day.

We will be honest this will take commitment. If you mess up, get sidetracked, or forget to study it is okay; just pick up where you left off and begin again. But remember, to get the best results you will want to commit and exercise the above-mentioned tools daily. Reading this devotional will not make you the perfect person, but it will help set the tone of your day and lead you in the direction to becoming a better child of God. So, we urge you to set aside daily time to concentrate on your Heavenly Father. We are confident that this book will help you transform your life for the better. We are not professing to have all the answers you need, but we are confessing to know a God that does!

To begin you will need:
- o   An open mind
- o   An open heart
- o   An open Bible

Authors' Suggestions
- o   Set practical goals for yourself
- o   Limit distractions (TV, phone, computer, etc.) to make the most of your personal study time
- o   Chart your progress

<u>**THE STRONGHOLD CONCEPT**</u>

We understand that the word stronghold is not used in our day-to-day interactions, so we would like to define this term before you read any further. The Merriam-Webster dictionary defines a stronghold as "a fortified place, or a place of security or survival." God's word describes a negative stronghold as a sin or transgression against the law (1 John 3:4), because it has exalted itself against the knowledge of God and must be pulled down (2 Corinthians 10:4-5).

There are three types of strongholds that you can read about in the Bible. First, there are **Physical** strongholds, such as walled cities, fortresses, or temples used as places of refuge or to thwart enemy attack (Numbers 13:17-19). Second, a **Holy** stronghold may include being led by the Spirit (Romans 8:14-17) or the fruit of the Spirit (Galatians 5:22-23). Third, there are **Wicked** strongholds, such as satan's control/influence (Ephesians 6:12) and the works of the flesh (Galatians 5:19-21, Colossians 3:5-9).

In this book we refer to strongholds as any negative force in your life that causes a separation in your relationship with God. It is a mental stumbling block that will "easily beset" or entangle you (Hebrews 12:1) so that your spiritual growth is stunted or interrupted. A stronghold may result in a habitual negative cycle that becomes a part of your lifestyle and the cycle repeats itself until you believe it is normal. It becomes who you are and how you look at and respond to situations, people, yourself, and God. For example, if you have a negative stronghold of doubt, not only will you doubt others, you may doubt yourself and doubt God to bring about positive changes in your life.

Strongholds can cause you to feel secure and protected when in fact you have shut yourself out from God and locked yourself in with the enemy. As you go through this devotional, realize satan has limited ability on this earth. He can only use tactics to attack your mind; so fight him with God's word during this spiritual warfare in order to defeat negative strongholds (Ephesians 6:10-18).

Enslaved Without a Master

Melanie Joyce Johnson

Satan plays this game with me

I give him the first move

He takes the reins and then I play

I'm just getting in the groove

He takes my turn, then steals the dice

The roll not in my favor

I jump through his hurdles, slide down his thoughts

His ideas I begin to savor

Do not pass go, but land in jail

My plight every move's disaster

I played a game meant for my shame

I'm enslaved without a master

Bonus round I'm gaining on him

I've almost made it closer

My victory, a few steps home for me

I lost, the game is over

The moral is don't play a game

That's already been won for you

Cause satan will come deceive your mind

Making up rules that were never true

Don't give away your pure mind

When satan runs so much faster

You'll leave behind, your soul entwined

Enslaved without a master.

WEEK ONE

IDENTITY THEFT

<u>Ephesians 6:10-12</u>

"Finally, my brethren, be strong in the Lord, and in the power of his might. Put on the whole armour of God, that ye may be able to stand against the wiles of the devil. For we wrestle not against flesh and blood, but against principalities, against powers, against the rulers of the darkness of this world, against spiritual wickedness in high places."

Introduction:

We live in a world where it is easy to diagnose the problems of others without ever examining ourselves. More than likely you can agree that you have found yourself working as an unlicensed Psychiatrist prescribing advice for the problems of others, yet rarely seeking help for your own troubles. Why is that? Sometimes it is because the sunglasses we wear seem to only reflect the lives of others; or maybe we are too fearful to expose the secrets of our own hearts.

Lesson:

How important is your identity? Have you ever heard of someone's identity being stolen? It can take a long time to repair one's credit after identity theft. Many who have experienced this describe it as a devastating feeling. Just like with physical identity theft, our spiritual identity can be stolen and we may not even be aware of it. For instance, some habits we have cultivated have robbed us of our spiritual purity.

Apostle Paul encourages us in 1 Corinthians 9:24, to run the race to win. Satan uses schemes against us, such as gossip, blame, or complaints to cause us to hide our faults. If we continue to mask our sins, we will never be able to win against satan. Have you been allowing satan to win in your life? You may not even recognize that he has a rule over you. Today, it is time to identify negative strongholds and begin freeing yourself from the Identity Thief.

As you have probably already guessed, his name is satan, and his motives are to kill, steal, and destroy (John 10:10). What pure thing has the robber taken from you and replaced with something contaminated? No one is without sin (Romans 3:23), and if you truly take a look within you can admit that you sin in some areas consistently. When you continue in sin you become separated from God. Therefore, it is essential to recognize the negative strongholds in your life, to remove them and reunite with the Lord. God provides scriptures to train you for spiritual warfare and once strongholds are identified you are able to use your armor to fight off the Identity Thief (Ephesians 6:11-12).

Let's break this down. When you think of a negative stronghold, what comes to mind? A negative stronghold can be described as an incorrect thinking pattern that molds itself into your way of belief. These strongholds have the ability to affect your feelings and control how you respond to situations. Negative strongholds will change who you are and how you behave. They may also present themselves as an inner child of your past, something in your background, or an episode that occurred that you have locked away in the back of your mind. Although put away, these former experiences feed and control certain behaviors today and manifest themselves as worry, depression, discouragement, or failure just to name a few. It is satan's job to make negative strongholds permanently control your life.

God knows your strongholds and He knows that satan uses them to ruin your relationship with Him. He wants you to protect your identity. Protection begins with 1) recognizing the strongholds in your life, 2) allowing God to work with you to tear them down and 3) distinguishing between the Savior and the enemy daily. During this process remember, God will not tempt you, but the enemy will (James 1:13). Today begins your journey to protect yourself against being the victim of spiritual identity theft. Satan is not happy because he wants to keep you in bondage. Break Free! Do not let satan and his negative strongholds win.

The list below identifies a few negative strongholds to help you determine what they look like. As you begin to detect them, do not become overwhelmed with the many you may have. Negative strongholds have been firmly planted by the enemy and his goal behind implanting them is to build a wall of resistance to the truth. God is ready to guide you to your breakthrough.

<u>Negative Stronghold Examples</u>:
Abusive behavior (emotional, mental, physical), Adultery, Boasting, Complacency, Debt, Doubt, False teaching, Fear, Fornication, Gossip, Greed, Hatred, Holding on to the past, Jealousy, Low self-esteem, Negativity, Pride, Pornography, Procrastination, Rehearsing hurts, Spirit of infirmity, Temper, Unforgiving (self or others), or Worry.

<u>**Reflective Prayer:**</u>

Dear God, as I start this purifying period, help me accept that I cannot do this alone. Thank you for my example, your Son, Jesus Christ. I ask that the Holy Spirit guide me on this journey. Lord, help me to be open first with you and secondly with myself so that I can identify the negative strongholds in my life. I ask for your forgiveness for my known and unknown sins. Please strengthen me in the areas where I am weak and aid me in becoming wise to satan's tactics. Without you God, I am nothing. I desire to place my complete trust in you. In Jesus' name, Amen.

<u>**Quote:**</u>

"Nobody can go back and start a new beginning, but anyone can start today and make a new ending."

- Maria Robinson

Day 1 "Lesson Reflection"

What kind of emotions do you think are involved
when someone's identity has been stolen? Would
these be the same for spiritual identity theft?

Daily Scripture Application: Psalm 32:7

Can you identify at least one negative issue that you deal with more than others? (Don't be ashamed to name more)

____
____
____
____
____
____
____
____
____
____
____
____
____
____
____
____

Daily Scripture Application: Hebrews 12:1

Day 3 "Lesson Reflection"

Reflecting on question 2, when does the negative stronghold appear? Does something trigger it?

____

____

____

____

____

____

____

____

____

____

____

____

____

____

____

____

____

____

Daily Scripture Application: 1 Peter 5:8

Day 4 "Lesson Reflection"

How has this stronghold damaged your relationship with God or others?

____
____
____
____
____
____
____
____
____
____
____
____
____
____
____
____
____

Daily Scripture Application: Acts 5:1-10

Day 5 "Lesson Reflection"

Start a list today of your negative strongholds. Over the course of this study, continue to document them as they are identified. Take note of when they appear and your actions toward them.

____

____

____

____

____

____

____

____

____

____

____

____

____

____

____

____

____

Daily Scripture Application: Proverbs 28:13

Shackled

HAND CUFFED

in Sin

Romans 7:14-23(NIV)

"We know that the law is spiritual; but I am unspiritual, sold as a slave to sin. I do not understand what I do. For what I want to do I do not do, but what I hate I do. And if I do what I do not want to do, I agree that the law is good. As it is, it is no longer I myself who do it, but it is sin living in me. I know that nothing good lives in me, that is, in my sinful nature. For I have the desire to do what is good, but I cannot carry it out. For what I do is not the good I want to do; no, the evil I do not want to do—this I keep on doing. Now if I do what I do not want to do, it is no longer I who do it, but it is sin living in me that does it. So I find this law at work: When I want to do good, evil is right there with me. For in my inner being I delight in God's law; but I see another law at work in the members of my body, waging war against the law of my mind and making me a prisoner of the law of sin at work within my members."

Introduction:

A letter from satan: "I saw you yesterday as you began your daily chores. You awoke without kneeling to pray. As a matter of fact, you didn't even bless your meals, or pray before going to bed last night. You are so unthankful, I like that about you. I cannot tell you how glad I am that you have not changed your way of living. Fool you are mine. Remember you and I have been going steady for years, and I still don't love you yet. As a matter of fact, I hate you, because I hate God. He kicked me out of heaven, and I'm going to use you as long as possible to pay him back. You see, Fool, GOD LOVES YOU and HE has great plans in store for you. But you have yielded your life to me, and I'm going to make your life a living hell. This will really hurt God. Thanks to you, I'm really showing Him who's boss in your life.

I've got some hot plans for us. This is just a letter of appreciation from me to you. I'd like to say "Thanks" for letting me use you for most of your foolish life. You are so gullible, I laugh at you. When you are tempted to sin, you give in. HA HA HA, you make me sick. Well, Fool, I have to let you go for now. I'll be back in a couple of seconds to tempt you again. If you were smart, you would run somewhere, confess your sins, and live for God with what little bit of life that you have left. It's not my nature to warn anyone, but don't get me wrong, I still hate you. It's just that you'd make a better fool for Christ."

P.S. If you love me, you won't share this.
(Borrowed)

<u>**Lesson:**</u>

Think deeply, did you find yourself in the fictional narrative above? If so, how do you feel? Does satan have you shackled in sin as the story describes? As you learned in the previous chapter, negative strongholds are weights that cause you to stand a guilty distance away from God. Satan wants to keep you shackled down knowing it will affect your relationship with the God-3 (that is, God The Father, God The Son, and God The Holy Spirit). To be shackled means to restrain in action or thought, to restrict, to be bound, chained, confined, cuffed, or held captive.

Let's dig a little deeper into the dangers of sin: *"Everyone who sins breaks the law. In fact, breaking the law is sin"* 1 John 3:4 (NIV). Also, *"When you sin, the pay you get is death"* Romans 6:23 (NIV). Sin is destructive and satan knows it. He was perfect before he sinned (Ezekiel 28:15); now his mission is to shackle you in sin and turn you against God. Sin is jail where satan rules over you. He opens your cell and closes it at his command. It is entrapment and his influence sets the restrictions. Satan wants you to imitate him and desire control, riches, and instant gratification so adamantly, that you take your focus off of God. He knows that if you trust in **your** abilities, in **your** agenda, and leave God's word, you too will sin.

The devil uses temptations that are appealing; he does not offer things that you have no desire for. He diverts the consequences of sin by creating a sense of comfort, yet sin should feel uncomfortable. Sin blinds you from your wrongdoings making the voice of God confusing. When you become accepting of sin in your life, you give satan power over you, thereby becoming numb to the consequences sin produces. The enemy is deceptive in all of his ways and he shackles you down by using the things God hates (Proverbs 6:16-19).

Satan makes hiding your sin from others easy because they are not always around you; but God knows all and sees all. God is aware of the negative strongholds in your life no matter how secretive you think they are. Are you playing around with the enemy and still trying to have a relationship with God? If so, realize that it won't work. Take a moment to examine yourself and see if there is a habitual sin that you are constantly facing. No, really take a moment and think about how this sin has shackled you. It lures you in, fills you up, snares you like a booby trap and locks you in.

Negative strongholds keep you in bondage. Bondage is a dark, vulnerable, place of restriction and one simple thought can place and keep you there if you don't do anything about it. For example, the reason you haven't forgiven yourself for something you've done years ago is because satan has created a negative stronghold of unforgiveness in your life and you have not escaped. You haven't recognized that God has forgiven you; so you haven't moved, forgiven, nor made any changes to get unshackled. Recognize this sin as a negative stronghold that has shackled you and you must *want* to get out of satan's trap.

Though you battle with sin, there should be a constant effort to correct it in your life; tell yourself, I don't want to be shackled anymore. When you sin, do not lose hope (1 John 3:3, Titus 2:14). Hope gives you something to live for and makes the trials you go through not as bad as they seem. Hope is a cure to your despair. You may mess up sometimes, but Jesus died so that you, with your imperfections, could live; and that's a reason to have hope!

Now it's your turn to write satan a letter (literally). Let him know that your relationship with him has ended! Once you finish writing that letter, shred it and throw it away, never to look at his evil influence over you any longer! It's Over! Don't give him any more power over you no matter what tricks he may use. Stand up to him and let him know he's called you his fool one too many times and you are surrendering and becoming a fool for Christ (1 Corinthians 4:10 NIV).

<u>**Reflective Prayer:**</u>

Father, I'm asking you to open my eyes and heart to the dangers of sin in my life. Lord, I need your guidance as I strive each day to identify negative strongholds in my life that have me shackled. I do recognize that sin separates me from you and I do not want to live a life disconnected from you; you are my ultimate power source. Teach me how to forgive myself. I admit Father that this journey has not been easy, but I choose not to give up. Today God, I need your help in writing a letter to satan that will keep him far away from me as I draw closer to you. Dependent on you I come, trusting you I give my hand; at your throne I release all negative strongholds in my life. In Jesus' name, Amen.

<u>**Quote:**</u>

"You leave old habits behind by starting out with the thought, 'I release the need for this in my life.'"

- Wayne Dyer

<u>*Day 6 "Lesson Reflection"*</u>

In what areas of your life have you been shackled by
satan?

____
____
____
____
____
____
____
____
____
____
____
____
____
____
____
____
____

Daily Scripture Application: Romans 1:28-32

Reflecting on the previous question, why have you given satan control over your life in this way?

____
____
____
____
____
____
____
____
____
____
____
____
____
____
____
____
____

Daily Scripture Application: Ephesians 2:1-7

<u>Day 8 "Lesson Reflection"</u>

Are you ashamed of those things that have you
shackled in sin? Why or why not?

Daily Scripture Application: Psalm 51

How does being in bondage to sin feel?

____

Daily Scripture Application: Romans 8:12-15

Day 10 "Lesson Reflection"

Why do you think that forgiveness of self and hope in God are necessary to defeat strongholds?

Daily Scripture Application: Psalm 147:11

WEEK THREE

SOLITARY CONFINEMENT

The Mind is a Terrible Thing to Waste

<u>Proverbs 23:7</u>
> "For as he thinketh in his heart, so is he."

Introduction:

My (Melanie) older brother is incarcerated. He spent the first few years of his 23-year sentence in Maximum Security, but moved to the Minimum Security side because of his good behavior. Recently the guards found contraband in his cell and they gave him a choice; either spend 3 days in solitary confinement or go back to the Maximum Security prison for 6 months. What do you think he chose? Knowing the horrible mental effects of going to the "hole," he chose the latter.

Imagine spending 23 hours a day alone in a cell. This extreme isolation for prolonged periods can cause anxiety; an impaired ability to think, concentrate, or even to remember. Just like a physical solitary confinement can cause mental distress, the effects of a spiritual solitary confinement can do the same. The mind is a terrible thing to waste and I think my brother knew this.

The mind is the only thing that the devil can use against you to persuade you to leave God and fall for him. He is not allowed to touch your physical body in any way, so his only mode of defeat is to infiltrate your mind and influence your thoughts. Your mind is the devil's playing field. Here he brings anxiety; here he persuades you to think you need something you don't; here instant gratification is nurtured.

When satan is allowed into your mind you set yourself up for a spiritual downfall. His aim is to make your habitual sins comfortable. He wants you to get so caught up in sin that you don't realize it's happening. He is subtly creating negative habits in your spiritual life. Has your mind gone to waste for the enemy? Have you found yourself rubbing shoulders with, sleeping with, or exchanging ideas with him? Your mind should be God's sanctuary instead of the devil's playground.

Habits, whether good or bad, begin in the mind. The longer a habit continues, the more it becomes ingrained and the harder it is to change. Satan knows this. Negative strongholds are bad habits birthed in negative thinking. It is your duty to replace your negative thoughts with positive ones. For instance, if you are tempted with lust, feed your mind with scriptures on purity and avoid compromising situations. If you are a habitual liar, begin to memorize what God's word says about honesty and truth and re-evaluate the root cause of your dishonesty. Until you do this, your negative behavior may never change.

If sin has been ruling your life, it is only because it is being fed into your mind. If you stop feeding the sin, it will die. Every time you dwell in a stronghold, satan is given the victory over your mind bringing you closer to him and moving you further from God.

A relationship with satan is like a dysfunctional mental prison; he creates a solitary confinement in your mind where he controls what comes in and goes out. Just like in the introduction story, the "enemy's hole" can bring great mental distress. It's up to you to poison him with positivity and scriptures like Jesus did in Matthew 4:1-11. Satan tried to tempt Jesus three times in the wilderness, by going after his mind, body, and spirit; but he did not win. Jesus defeated satan, and so can you! He had up a positive stronghold (God's Word) and it caused satan to flee. If you want him to flee from your life, remember, **God** holds the key. Use Him to get you out!

You only have one mind; don't let it go to waste for the enemy's use. Dwell on the scriptures daily, so satan can have less time to play around with your thoughts. Transformed thinking gives birth to complete change. Remember, God is still at work in your life so don't give up, no matter how tough it gets (Philippians 1:6).

<u>**Reflective Prayer:**</u>

Dear Lord, thank you so much for this avenue of prayer where I can come to you and tell you everything that is on my mind. I pray that the Holy Spirit encourages me to develop the mind of Christ. In the past, I have been doing things my way or even someone else's way and my thoughts led me down the wrong path. I have been sadly dwelling in a spiritual solitary confinement and I need your help to get out. Lord, I do not want to give my mind over to satan anymore. I want to be released from his prison and think freely as the child you have created me to be. It is my prayer now, that I bind my mind and thoughts to you and allow your perfect Will to be done in my life. Thank you in advance. In the precious name of Jesus I pray, Amen.

<u>**Quote:**</u>

"Once we start thinking and saying what we really want then our minds automatically shift and pull us in that direction."

- Jim Rohn

How often do you find yourself involved in stinking thinking?

Daily Scripture Application: Philippians 2:5

Day 12 "Lesson Reflection"

In what ways have you allowed satan to control your mind?

Daily Scripture Application: Luke 22:1-4

Day 13 "Lesson Reflection"

What negative thoughts about yourself or others must you remove?

Daily Scripture Application: Ephesians 4:22-24

Day 14 "Lesson Reflection"

What steps will you take to actively annihilate satan?

Daily Scripture Application: Matthew 4:1-11

What benefits are there to having the mind of Christ?

Daily Scripture Application: Isaiah 26:3

WEEK FOUR
PHONE HOME

Power of Prayer

<u>Psalm 118:5-6</u>

"I called upon the Lord in distress: the Lord answered me, and set me in a large place. The Lord is on my side; I will not fear: what can man do to me?"

Introduction:

When a person is arrested and taken to jail they are initially allowed to make one phone call. Many times they will call a parent, guardian, preacher, close friend, or someone they KNOW to come bail them out. In his prayer to God, (Psalm 118:5-6) David called on the Lord in distress and He answered. So many times we call on the wrong people to bail us out of our troubles when God wants us to call upon Him. The benefit of prayer is that you can phone home to God more than one time and He will always answer.

Lesson:

Prayer is our most underused privilege. Sometimes we forget that the connection between heaven and earth starts on our knees in prayer. Prayer is one of the most vulnerable positions to be in. It is us telling God, that we are not sufficient, wise, or strong enough to do it all by ourselves. Prayer is not the place to boast, but to beg mercy. It is not the place to be super intelligent nor filled with spiritual jargon, but to be humbled before Christ; Prayer is submission to God, who is the only person that CAN do what we cannot do. Breaking negative strongholds is a continual journey that will take much prayer.

You may think, I've been praying and it doesn't seem to work for me. We want to encourage you; do not lose heart. The Word instructs us to pray without ceasing (1 Thessalonians 5:17), so it's perfectly okay to pray for one situation many times. At just the moment you feel like giving up, that next prayer could be the one that works. Take these next three steps to expand what you have already been doing. *Check* the Record of how God has answered in the past; *Ask* for the removal of the stronghold, and *believe* it will be done, by the power of God working through your prayers.

Check (Genesis 18:14, Jeremiah 32:27). God's track record has shown us the power of prayer all throughout scripture. Prayer has conquered physical death (2 Kings 4:3-37). Prayer has changed the weather forecast (James 5:17). Prayer has allowed people to overcome their enemies (Psalm 6:9-10). Prayer has cast out demons (Mark 9:29). Prayer has broken shackles and prison doors (Acts 16:25-26). Prayer has also resulted in healing (James 5:14-16). If biblical prayers can do that, just imagine what the power of prayer will do to the negative strongholds in your life! Check the record of what He's done for you.

Ask (Matthew 7:7-11). Do you believe that God will give you the things you ask for? Do you believe He knows how to bless you? Of course He does. He is Almighty God! He is patiently waiting for you to talk to Him. Your prayer does not have to be a perfectly crafted speech. Just start talking. Show God you are ready to witness the power of prayer in your life by asking boldly for the things you desire (Psalm 37:4). Request that He remove negative strongholds from your life.

Believe (1 John 5:14-15). Have you ever had trouble believing in God to answer your prayers? Many have felt that same way. We have not received the results we wanted or God didn't answer in enough time; so we stop believing in Him. Matthew 21:22 says if you ask God anything in prayer, _believing,_ you shall receive. That is power! Your Father would not ask you to pray, if He did not already have you in mind on His prayer list. He would not ask you to talk with Him, if He was not going to provide a way out (1 Corinthians 10:13); but you must believe! His answers are always on time. Believe that He will remove your negative strongholds.

Prayer is power and God has that power. He wants you to tap into it so that you can be the vessel to display that power to the world. All it takes is checking His record, asking Him what you want to see happen in your life and believing it will be done. Phone home today and ask the Lord to take away negative strongholds from your life. Never let a guilty heart keep you from praying. Remember you are forgiven and the power of God working in your life is waiting to be unleashed!

Reflective Prayer:

Dear Father, I pray believing! I pray deeply and faithfully. I know you are capable of getting me out of my mess because I've seen you do it in the past. Forgive me Lord for those times that I've run to others to discuss my problems instead of calling on you to help me. Forgive me for thinking I can handle it, and then when I mess up, blame you for not being there when and how I thought you should. I ask that you purify my heart, so that when I come to you, I not only acknowledge the power that prayer has in my life, I act on it. I am not perfect, but I know that if I am trying daily to renew myself in your Word, I can and will become more spiritually wise and mature. I pray believing. In Jesus' name, Amen.

Quote:

"Any concern too small to be turned into a prayer is too small to be made into a burden."

- Corrie ten Boom

Day 16 "Lesson Reflection"

Have you ever doubted the power of your prayers?
Why or why not?

____

____

____

____

____

____

____

____

____

____

____

____

____

____

____

____

____

____

Daily Scripture Application: Mark 11:24

Day 17 "Lesson Reflection"

Name people that you routinely call on when you have a problem. Was God on that list? What would you need to rearrange in your life to make Him priority?

Daily Scripture Application: Isaiah 65:24

Day 18 "Lesson Reflection"

When checking God's record in your life, did you recall any prayers that He answered? How did you respond?

____
____
____
____
____
____
____
____
____
____
____
____
____
____
____
____
____
____

Daily Scripture Application: Jeremiah 33:3

Have you asked God to bail you out of your spiritual prison yet? Reread the scriptures that have been given on prayer. Find 3 additional scriptures that demonstrate how He can deliver you from your stronghold.

____

____

____

____

____

____

____

____

____

____

____

____

____

____

____

Daily Scripture Application: Psalm 18:19-21

Day 20 "Lesson Reflection"

Note strongholds that you want to put into God's hands. Write a prayer of faith and journal when and how God answers your prayer.

Daily Scripture Application: 2 Peter 2:9a

PAROLE

Submitting and Resisting

Submitting and Resisting

<u>James 4:7</u>

"Submit yourselves therefore to God. Resist the devil, and he will flee from you."

Introduction:

Many prisoners sentenced to life hope for parole. Parole, although it still restricts in some capacity, presents the possibility of life outside of a jail cell. At the same time parole causes one to be on guard, careful, but hopeful that walking the right path will keep them from having to return to prison. What about our spiritual lives? Are we as careful in our walk as paroled inmates?

Lesson:

Satan has made sin so easy that it becomes comfortable and brings about great pain to depart from it. In 1 Peter 5:8, God warns us of the motive of satan. *"Be sober, be vigilant; because your adversary the devil, as a roaring lion, walketh about, seeking whom he may devour."* Satan is going to do all he can to keep you from reaching your goal of spiritual freedom. He will tempt you in areas where he knows you are weak. He will try to convince you that you are a failure because you mess up sometimes. He will make you think it is too hard to do right.

Has satan fled from you because of the commitment you have made to God, or do you find that you two are still meeting at the same place and same time, everyday? Have you ever found yourself bribing God to get you out of a bad situation; delivering promises such as, "Lord if you get me out of this one, I promise I will give you more of my time;" or "Lord, I know I've asked you to bring me through this same thing once or twice before, but I **really** promise this time that if you let this cup pass from me I will never ever get caught up in this again." Perhaps we have all said these phrases because it is not always easy to submit to God and resist the devil.

Consider yourself on spiritual parole. You are released from the prison of being shackled in negative strongholds. You must now make wise decisions so that you don't end up making promises to God that you cannot keep, or worse end up in jail again. Most paroled inmates revert back to old habits because their parole officer is not always by their side. However, God is your parole officer, and He is aware of everything that is going on in your life (Psalm 121:4). Before sliding back into old comfort zones, realize that your parole officer is watching. Although you are on spiritual parole, don't confuse your freedom with independence to do whatever you desire. God is watching even though you don't see

Him. He is looking to see if you remember His word when the walk gets challenging.

Jesus, your perfect example has left steps for you to follow in. He understands that when times get tough it may be easy to give in to satan, yet He opposed the devil many times to make him flee (Matthew 4, Mark 8:33, 1 John 3:8-9). If you want satan to flee from you, submit to God and resist the devil as mentioned in James 4:7. You do this by surrendering your will to God's will and not giving the enemy the time of day. Because of Christ's victory, you are now victorious. Embrace that thought and follow in the footsteps of Jesus (1 Peter 2:21)!

You are not alone in this journey. When Christ ascended into heaven after defeating sin and death, God dispatched His Spirit. The Holy Spirit is your guide. He comforts, convicts of sin, and guides you away from strongholds (John 14:16-18; 16:5-15). At this point, satan will remind you of those places of comfort. Listen to the Spirit instead. Do not suppress Him (Ephesians 4:30). The Spirit is working with you, not against you so use Him to your advantage.

To resist the devil is to stand your ground against him. There is no way he can defeat you without your consent. Will you submit to the Lord and resist the enemy? Remember, your parole officer will never leave nor forsake you. The choice is yours!

Reflective Prayer:

Dear Lord, time after time you have come to my rescue only for me to end back up in the same mess. Lord, I am sorry for taking your forgiveness for granted. As I am striving to be a better servant, please guide me because I cannot make it on my own. Allow your Holy Spirit to stay with and strengthen me. God, I recognize that you are patient with me even when I make promises that you know I won't keep. Thank you for loving me and holding me accountable for my actions. I'm ready to step out on faith **with** you. In Jesus' name I pray, Amen.

Quote:

"It is not only what we do, but also what we do not do, for which we are accountable."

- Moliere

Day 21 "Lesson Reflection"

What areas of your life are you constantly running
back to?

____

____

____

____

____

____

____

____

____

____

____

____

____

____

____

____

Daily Scripture Application: Galatians 5:17-18

What is causing you to retreat to those areas of comfort?

Daily Scripture Application: Romans 6:16-19

Day 23 "Lesson Reflection"

When you think about God being your parole officer, how does that make you feel? Are you more cognizant of your attitude/actions toward sin?

Day 24 "Lesson Reflection"

Are you confessing and confronting your sins or reporting and repeating them?

Daily Scripture Application: Psalm 32:5

Day 25 "Lesson Reflection"

The Holy Spirit has been left as a comforter and a guide. How are you placing your trust in Him during this journey?

Daily Scripture Application: Proverbs 3:5

WEEK SIX
REHABILITATION

<u>I John 4:4</u>

"Ye are of God, little children, and have overcome them: because greater is he that is in you, than he that is in the world."

Introduction:

Rehabilitation is a specific therapy aimed at improving health. No one really likes to go through rehab because it takes work. It is used to bring one to complete restoration after an emotional, psychological, or physical illness has been treated. People go to rehab to regain their physical health, but in this lesson we focus on restoring your spiritual health.

Lesson:

It's time to see the Doctor. Satan has used every trick in the book to keep you sick. Remember he lost you; so now every scheme he knows he is going to use to get you back. Spiritually, he (satan) has tried to fill you up on stronghold drugs, and every time you try to wean yourself off you go through withdrawal. You withdraw from your family, your supporters, and God. You end up neglecting the very thing your body needs, Jesus. Use the Doctor's word as the antidote to bring your mind back to its spiritual readiness and to defend yourself against satan.

Christ is the remedy for your spiritual illness. Through Him, you are able to endure anything that comes your way. Through Him, you are made new. He is the strength that you lean on. Don't just read these words; we encourage you to truly surrender and let Him heal you. God's clinic (the Bible) is open 24/7. He, Jesus, and the Holy Spirit can deliberate and prescribe the best practical treatment for your stronghold habit. Step into rehab and begin to say goodbye to the pain that strongholds have caused.

Here's a simple method:
- o <u>Go to the Doctor</u>: If you're hurting or sick you normally go to the doctor for the answers. Why? Because doctors are trustworthy and have proven to heal. The Doctor's office is not the place to give your own opinion of what you think will heal you. God knows what to do and will instruct you wisely. The Doctor has never lost anyone that He's operated on. He can be trusted. His advice is backed up by scriptural testimony and research. Many have called on Him and been delivered. Others have touched the hem of His garment and been healed. And we read about the one who was raised from the

dead. Can you testify of what He's brought you through?

o <u>Practice the Doctor's Orders</u>: Recovery requires that you re-program your way of life. You can't keep doing the same old things and expect new changes to occur. The remedy prescribed by the Doctor will be frequent intake of the scriptures. Begin exercising your mind by examining yourself against the Word (2 Corinthians 13:5). If what you see in yourself doesn't match up with what the scripture says, make the necessary changes in your life. This may hurt at first, because it's taking something away that you found comfort in; but reading and applying scripture fills that empty space and builds you back up. Just like an antibiotic, each scripture you read will shatter the stronghold that infected you.

o <u>Frequent Follow-up with the Doctor</u>: Write down areas that still need improvement. What areas are still causing you pain? Record where you see yourself continuing to fall. (Refer to Lesson 1 to see if there are new strongholds recognized in your life). It will also help remove the issues of your past that hinder your spiritual relationship with God. Let the Doctor know constantly how you feel—through prayer. Continual follow-up will prove to be satisfying to your soul.

Spiritual rehabilitation provides great benefits that shatter your strongholds. *Physically*, you regain liveliness. You are purged from the sluggishness of strongholds. Your appearance is brighter, as you start taking off the dark mask of sin. *Emotionally*, you get back in touch with those long lost positive feelings about yourself that God placed in you at the beginning. You will love yourself, and it will show because you will no longer attack and immerse yourself in strongholds that once kept you in chains of gloom. *Mentally*, your thinking improves. You will think the way God does about your strongholds, and you will want to change. You will think about yourself in a different light and satan's influence will have less control over your life. *Spiritually*, your relationship with God will be restored. You will be stronger in your walk of faith because He is with you. You will have overcome stronghold indulgence and your spirit will thank you for feeding it with the fruit of God's word.

The Doctor has endowed you with the power to defeat your strongholds. You can overcome the ill effects of negative strongholds (1 John 4:4)! Remove all doubts and fears and surrender to the Doctor that restores.

<u>**Reflective Prayer:**</u>

Dear Lord, I give you all the thanks, credit, and glory for restoring me back to my spiritual and mental health. Help me to continue to renew my mind by surrendering my thoughts to your will. Rehabilitation is a tough process, but realizing that I won't be defeated, I won't be in despair, I won't be destroyed, and I won't be forsaken makes the process more meaningful. God, I know that I am not perfect and am likely to be led away again; but my Perfect Doctor can heal me. I'm praying now for my speedy recovery. Thank you again Lord for helping me to serve you and not satan. I am indebted to you for your faith in my recovery. In Jesus' name I pray, Amen.

<u>**Quote:**</u>

"Don't let the fear of the time it will take to accomplish something stand in the way of your doing it. The time will pass away. We might just as well put that passing time to the best possible use."

- Anonymous

Are you aware of the areas of weakness that may lead you towards a relapse? (Name them)

Daily Scripture Application: Psalm 71:20-21

Day 27 "Lesson Reflection"

What fears do you have in giving up your strongholds? Are you holding on to them and not going to therapy?

____

____

____

____

____

____

____

____

____

____

____

____

____

____

____

Daily Scripture Application: 2 Timothy 1:7

What withdrawal symptoms (i.e., anger, bitterness, isolation) have you experienced after trying to get rid of stronghold drugs?

Daily Scripture Application: 1 Peter 1:14-16

Day 29 "Lesson Reflection"

Imagine breaking your strongholds into tiny pieces;
now break them down into who, what, when, where,
and why you engage in them. Shatter them with
prayer.

Daily Scripture Application: Philippians 4:6-7

Day 30 "Lesson Reflection"

Name some of the benefits you hope to gain from spiritual rehabilitation.

Daily Scripture Application: 2 Peter 1:3-9

WEEK SEVEN
TIME TO WORK

Practicing and Creating Good Habits

Romans 12:2

"And be not conformed to this world: but be ye transformed by the renewing of your mind, that ye may prove what is that good, and acceptable, and perfect, will of God."

Introduction:

You are probably familiar with the cliché, "Practice makes perfect!" It's a saying that has been in existence for many years. Does practice *really* make perfect? If I practice shooting free throws everyday, at the same place and the same time, will I be a *perfect* free throw shooter, or am I practicing and creating a habit that will enhance my basketball skills? The point is, we consciously and unconsciously repeat habits daily: studying God's word, preparing for work, fixing food for the family, or engaging in positive and negative conversations. These habits not only affect us but they affect those who witness our behaviors.

We must understand that the strongholds we departed from were *negative* habits that we mastered and were comfortable performing. Satan loved that those habits were frequently practiced and modeled to others. Knowing how he operates, and knowing what God wants, we should strive to create and practice good habits instead; those that will bring God glory and not shame. So, are you ready to practice positive habits?

<u>**Lesson:**</u>

Satan is not pleased with you. Since you ended your relationship with him he has not been able to get over hearing those words, "It's Over." He is not thrilled that you are at a point in your life where the same old negative habits have become annoying to you and practicing and creating new habits is now something you desire. God, however, *is* proud of you! He sees you growing spiritually from milk to meat and transforming into a mature Christian.

Application of God's word is crucial to defeating negative strongholds. For everything you are dealing with there is a word from the Lord to help you overcome it! Paul encourages us in Philippians 4:8 to think on *"whatsoever things are true, whatsoever things are honest, whatsoever things are just, whatsoever things are pure, whatsoever things are lovely, and whatsoever things are of good report."* Transforming your thinking acts as the fuel for your positive habits. Daily you should practice works that please God and not yourself. You do this by adapting a realistic routine into your lifestyle that forces you to replace negative things with positive ones.

Since lesson one, you have been listing negative strongholds in your life. Your list has probably gotten longer as you are becoming more honest with yourself and allowing the Holy Spirit to reveal more strongholds to you. Look at your list. Are these habits working for you, or against you? Are they damaging your relationship with God? Try this short exercise. There are no right or wrong answers; fill in the blank with a positive opposite to the negative:

    o   Replace fear with

    ____

    o   Replace negativity with

    ____

    o   Replace pain with

    ____

    o   Replace bitterness with

    ____

Now, find a scripture to match or support the answer you provided. This will further reinforce the positive word you found.

You can reverse the negatives in your life. Because of the work it takes to do the right thing, it's easy to say, I can't do this. I can't go any further. I can't seem to do the right thing. Have you been guilty of a CAN'T attitude? The word can't places invisible handcuffs on your spirit. Have faith that the Lord can mold you from any point in your life to be the person He needs you to be. Don't leave God; He wants to help you stay unshackled. Alone we are not strong enough, but with God **all things are possible**

(Matthew 19:26). It all starts with a shift from "I can't with satan" to "I will with God." Repeat Philippians 4:13, "I *can* *do* *all* *things* *through* *Christ* *which* *strengthens* *me*" until your actions show you truly believe it! Today, reverse your cant's and <u>C</u>hange <u>A</u>ll <u>N</u>egative <u>T</u>houghts by practicing new, positive habits!

<u>**Reflective Prayer:**</u>

My God, My God, I see myself in this lesson. I have some repetitive habits that have been causing me to stand a guilty distance away from you. Lord, help me in the areas where I am weak. I need your help to remove habits in my life that bring you shame. Lord, please strengthen me to create habits that will help others see you through me. I am ready for my spiritual transformation. I stand ready to be used by you and I refuse to give satan any more of me. I recognize that I cannot do this alone, so I am pleading Lord for your help. I am asking you to guide my feet and hold my hand. Because I am in you, I know that I can endure all things through Christ; help me to grasp that concept and apply it to my life. I love you so much Lord. In Jesus' name I pray, Amen.

<u>**Quote:**</u>

"Motivation is what gets you started. Habit is what keeps you going."

– Jim Rohn

Day 31 "Lesson Reflection"

Do you recognize negative habits within yourself that disgust you?

Daily Scripture Application: Romans 7:14-25

Has your thinking been a hindrance to releasing your negative habits into God's hands? How so?

____

____

____

____

____

____

____

____

____

____

____

____

____

____

____

____

____

Daily Scripture Application: 1 Peter 5:7

Day 33 "Lesson Reflection"

Why is it necessary to not conform to the habits of the world? Do you find yourself blending in with the world?

Daily Scripture Application: Romans 12:1-2

Day 34 "Lesson Reflection"

Knowing that God will assist you, what will you do
to start a positive habit?

Daily Scripture Application: Psalm 121:1-2

Day 35 "Lesson Reflection"

What I CAN'T statements will you turn into I CAN statements?

Daily Scripture Application: Philippians 4:13

WEEK EIGHT
STRONG SUPPORT GROUP

<u>Matthew 18:20</u>
"For where two or three are gathered together in my name, there am I in the midst of them."

Introduction:

If you name it, there may be a support group for it. Whether it is for dealing with trauma, alcoholism, abuse, weight loss, overcoming phobias or addictions, you will definitely find a support circle to help you overcome your past negative experiences. Support groups serve many purposes such as receiving encouragement from others, developing positive coping skills, finding unique friendships, and connecting you with many helpful resources. We want to inspire you to identify a person and/or several people to be your Spiritual Accountability Partner (S.A.P.). As you are overcoming and breaking free from strongholds, wouldn't it be nice to have a strong spiritual support group to lean on?

Lesson:

Do you remember the song "Lean On Me?" Bill Withers wrote *"Just call on me brother when you need a hand, we all need somebody to lean on. I just might have a problem that you'll understand, we all need somebody to lean on.*" Some of us cannot even sing those lyrics because we have allowed our strongholds to keep us isolated from others. For far too long you have been leaning on your stronghold for comfort. No one knows you're hurting or ever sees that you're struggling, because you've become so skilled at keeping others out and away from your life. Outside of the Lord, whom do you have to lean on?

You are not in this alone. God desires to be in a relationship with us and said it is not good that man should be alone (Genesis 2:18). So many times we only apply this verse to marriage. The word man in this verse refers to mankind and the helpmeet designed for mankind is someone who aids. This verse can literally read "it is not good for mankind to be alone, so I will create someone that will aid them." Our need for fellowship and friendship is strong and having a support network that you can lean on would be ideal as you break negative strongholds.

In order to receive help you have to open up and say that you need it. No one can read your mind. You will have to call on a brother or a sister to help you defeat your strongholds. Your S.A.P. should strengthen and edify you on a consistent basis, but how can they do this if they don't know? Ask the Lord to help you overcome any guilty feelings you may have about sharing your struggles with others. Being vulnerable in this area will aid in your victory over satan! Likewise, pray that He will reveal your S.A.P. to you and trust that He will place him or her on your heart and in your path at just the right time. When your S.A.P. is revealed begin sharing your spiritual goals with them.

Your S.A.P. will know when you are suffering because s/he will feel your pain. First Corinthians 12:26 states, *"And whether one member suffer, all the members suffer with it."* Being entangled in a stronghold makes us all suffer. An active support group will help relieve the suffering and find ways to heal the hurts. Your S.A.P. is not there to erase your errors, but rather to help you confront your mistakes and highlight your strengths that will aid you in destroying the devil with his schemes.

Likewise, your S.A.P. will not always tell you what you want to hear. S/he will be honest with you because ultimately they want to see you overcome your strongholds. S.A.P.s are there to correct you when you are wrong and lead you down the right road to recovery. They will not be jealous of your breakthrough, but know that Jesus is the reason behind it. When you are sick, your S.A.P. should be by your side. When you are falling, they should pick you up. When you are slipping in your day-to-day routines, they should hold you accountable to the spiritual goals you have set for yourself because it's all about carrying each other's burdens (Galatians 6:2). Your S.A.P is ready and willing to help you break up with the enemy! Look around; there may be someone in your life already doing these things. They might be a potential S.A.P.! As you pray and prepare to develop a strong support group to join you on your journey to experiencing freedom, remember the words *"lean on me when you're not strong, and I'll be your friend, I'll help you carry on. For, it won't be long, till I'm gonna need somebody to lean on!"*

<u>**Reflective Prayer:**</u>

Dear Lord, while I am defeating these negative strongholds, reveal to me who it is in the flesh that can help me on my journey. I thank you for Jesus who is a friend that sticks closer than a brother. God, please guide me toward a spiritual partner who will continue to hold me accountable to the spiritual goals I have set for myself and use me as a vessel of your encouragement, love, and care for those you send my way. As I learn to discern the support group that I need around me, keep me positive and prayerful, acknowledging that you are the first person that I will go to in my time of need. In Jesus' name I pray, Amen.

<u>**Quote:**</u>

"We must remember that one determined person can make a significant difference, and that a small group of determined people can change the course of history."
- Sonia Johnson

What does a support group look like to you and what are its functions?

Daily Scripture Application: James 5:13-16

Day 37 "Lesson Reflection"

Do you have a support group? If not, what has kept
you from creating one?

____

____

____

____

____

____

____

____

____

____

____

____

____

____

____

____

____

Daily Scripture Application: Galatians 6:2

How would a support group help you overcome your negative strongholds?

____
____
____
____
____
____
____
____
____
____
____
____
____
____
____
____

Daily Scripture Application: Hebrews 10:24

Begin to pray for God to send a S.A.P. your way. What spiritual goals would you like to share with them? (If you already have a S.A.P. thank God for them and continue to share your experiences with them.)

Daily Scripture Application: 1 Corinthians 1:10

Are you available to be a S.A.P. for someone else?
Why or why not?

Daily Scripture Application: Romans 12:10

EXPERIENCING FREEDOM

<u>Romans 6:22</u>

"But now being made free from sin, and become servants to God, ye have your fruit unto holiness, and the end everlasting life."

Introduction:

What is freedom? Have you ever experienced it? What does it feel like, sound like, look like? You have been released. Don't read over that so fast, you've been released!! What a relief it is not to be bound anymore by satan! There's no turning back now; why would you want to anyway, You're FREE. The air is fresher on this side, wouldn't you agree?

Lesson:

Daily, Jesus Christ has a one-on-one chat with God interceding on your behalf. He's pleading with God to forgive you of your wrongs and to set you free. Jesus won't leave you hanging. Jesus paid a debt He did not owe, and now continues to work for you, ensuring that you remain free! How does it make you feel to know God loves you that much?

God extends freedom to you through His Son, Jesus. So what does freedom in Christ mean? Freedom in Christ means you have Grace. Grace is a gift from God. You receive grace because of Christ's sacrifice for you. It was not deserved, but given anyway. Freedom in Christ *does not* mean God has given you the liberty to do "whatever you want." Freedom in Christ means you can pray to God about anything, anywhere, and at any time you want. You are free to have a relationship with God that you don't have to hide.

Are you willing to make a sacrifice for Christ and put away your negative strongholds for good? Do you desire to freely live with Him by being obedient to His word? You no longer have to walk around being a slave to a stronghold, but you can be a servant of righteousness through freedom (Romans 6:22).

It's important to note that if you choose to hold on to your negative strongholds then you are choosing NOT to be free. You are choosing bondage. You are choosing a complicated, negative relationship with satan. When you surrender to God, you have no shackles, no handcuffs, and no chains holding you down. John 8:36 states, *"If the Son therefore shall make you free, ye shall be free indeed."* That is a promise. Jesus has not gone back on His word; but it is up to you to trust Him. Are you trusting Him to set you free from worries, guilt, selfishness, anger, lying, fornication, adultery, fear, smoking, profanity, doubt, gossip, and other negative strongholds that have held you back from a sacred relationship with God?

At this point you must know your limits. You must remember those things that triggered sinful thoughts and actions and don't go there! Remove tempting things from your view. Don't go to those places that conjure up evil or depressing feelings within you. It is that simple. Once you know your limits, it's easier not to exceed them. Also, it is imperative to remember the practices given in this book. Acknowledge what held you bound and train your mind to focus on doing what's right and pleasing to God. Think of the scripture(s) that resonated with you the most in this journey and meditate on that verse to make it a part of your daily fight against the enemy. Remain constant in prayer and surround yourself with positive supporters and encouragers.

You are free through God's truths (John 17:17). You are free through Christ (Hebrews 2:14-15). You are free through the Holy Spirit (John 16:13). Persistently Pull Down negative strongholds (2 Corinthians 10:3-5) and never forget the power God has endowed you with to defeat negative strongholds in your life (2 Timothy 1:7). Don't allow satan to win, remember he can only go as far as you allow him.

There is no turning back. Take a deep breath and claim your freedom… It's Over!

Reflective Prayer:

Dear Lord, as I reflect on my life and my actions that have been revealed to me through reading this book, I pray that you will use me now for your glory. Through your mighty power I ask that you forgive me for leaving my loving relationship with you to be entangled in a dysfunctional and destructive relationship with satan. God you are my first love, and as I release these negative strongholds and embrace freedom, I believe that you will keep your promise and welcome me back with open arms. I acknowledge that it is because of Your grace and mercy, Jesus' sacrifice, and the Holy Spirit's guidance that I am able to completely free myself from the yoke of bondage. Thank you, Lord, for bringing me to a new point in my walk where I can be free in you. Thank you for your love, thank you for your care, thank you for your strength. I claim freedom. In Jesus' precious name I pray. Amen.

Quote:

"If the Son therefore shall make you free, ye shall be free indeed."

– Jesus Christ

Write a prayer of thanks for what God has revealed to
you through this journey.

____

____

____

____

____

____

____

____

____

____

____

____

____

____

____

____

____

Daily Scripture Application: Psalm 136:1

Day 42 "Lesson Reflection"

Write a prayer for faith to continue to overcome your strongholds.

____

____

____

____

____

____

____

____

____

____

____

____

____

____

____

____

Daily Scripture Application: Matthew 17:20

Day 43 "Lesson Reflection"

Write a prayer about the wholeness you've received through God's forgiveness and forgiveness of yourself.

Day 44 "Lesson Reflection"

Write a prayer about your value and worth to God.

Daily Scripture Application: 1 Peter 2:9

Day 45 *"Lesson Reflection"*

Write a prayer of freedom for breaking negative
strongholds in your life.

Daily Scripture Application: 2 Corinthians 10:3-5

The Last Dance

Melanie Joyce Johnson

I did a two-step shuffle
Stanky leggin, tootsie
rolling
Found out how to duggie
with a running man hustle
with the devil this year
And he serenaded me in sin
As I waltzed my way to
worry
Did a jealous jump and jive
As my mind taps out this
story
But I'm leaving the dance
floor
Where he flipped and dipped
me daily
I'm fleeing for my life and
I'm on my way to safety
And, YES I'm leaving
My complaints at the door
And, NO
I'm not gone cry
I'm not gone cry
I'm not gone shed no tear
Cause God knows that river
would just overflow with
my fear
So, so long troubles make
your home in the wind

You can save that last dance
because that one won't get
me in
And I'm so thankful satan
for the hateration this year
It gives me my motivation
you hear
So while you just sitting
possessed by the powers of
this world
I'll be sitting pretty
Purposed by His power
unfurled
Because I'm your never
ending story as long as I
follow His command
Cause I talk about Jesus the
one and only story ever
known to save man
Soooo I'll keep standing
with my head held high
While you keep hating as
His blessings pass you bye
bye bye
I won't be ashamed for
skipping a beat,
For missing my steps, for
tripping over my feet

I'm going into the next with
a spiritual new new
I got my eyes fixed so
Happy New You
Cause I'll be working on
new me
And we've become good
friends
My old self shoes don't
match my new self trends
Which warrants change
A change that God
wouldn't want to erase
The change that won't make
my Father ashamed
The change that He was
waiting for me to proclaim
The change from a dance
that only left me insane
See what looked like crazy to
y'all
Is the joke me and my
Father have been laughing
about all along

So I'm gone,
Holla, peace out, and deuces
If you need to get at me to
handle our truces
You know where to find me
Not on that same dance
floor
Where I lost my footing
But somewhere in that
vineyard
Where I'll be putting
My best foot forward
And Lord knows I can't
wait to get there
The time is tick tocking and
I'm on my way there
So Satan save your last
dance for somebody who
cares
I'll be long gone while
you're stuck in your stares

<u>**Statement of Encouragement:**</u>

Congratulations! You have survived this challenging journey from breaking up with satan to reconciling your relationship with God. We pray that you've seen some great changes in your life and walk with the Lord. This is not the end of the journey; it is just the beginning! Satan will try every trick in his arsenal to influence you to turn back to your comfortable seat of sin. Don't do it! You've come this far, so keep on moving. The Son of God has died to set you free, *so be free indeed* (John 8:36). Don't willingly put the shackles back on and give your life back over to satan.

It's Over! We can't stress it enough! Keep the old relationship with satan buried and experience freedom in your relationship with the LORD!!

Blessings,

      Melanie Joyce Johnson & Shanita R. Jones

<u>**God's Plan of Salvation**</u> **(1 Corinthians 15:1-4)**

Hear the Gospel (Romans 10:17), **Believe** the Gospel (Hebrews 11:6), **Repent** of sins by having a change of heart and a change of mind (Luke 13:3), **Confess** faith in Christ Jesus (Matthew 10:32-33), and be **Baptized** in water (Mark 16:15-16) for the remission of sins.

To GOD Be
All The Glory